# the lunch box

# the
# lunch
# box

Kate McMillan & Sarah Putman Clegg

weldon**owen**

# contents

think outside
the (lunch) box

**OK, we're all living in the real world.** Few parents have
the time and energy to pack a new, exciting lunch for their children
each day. It's enough of a challenge getting breakfast and dinner
on the table. But if you're stuck in a lunch box rut, this book can
jump-start your imagination without adding to your workload.

Some of these recipes will be much-needed additions to your
weekly rotation. Others you may simply not have considered as
lunchtime material, and they will help you use items already on
hand in new and thrilling ways. Plus, you'll discover some brilliant
ideas about presenting lunch food so it's more fun to pack and
eat. You may be surprised at the variety of foods you can entice
your child to eat by simply making them look, well, irresistible.

Another key to lunch-packing success? Preparation is everything.
Investing just a little time in advance—like making a batch
of egg salad on Sunday or setting out packing supplies the night
before—is much more efficient than starting from scratch every
day, saving you time and preventing brain drain on hectic mornings.
If what goes into the lunch box is an afterthought, it's going to taste
like an afterthought. But with its smart strategies and practical
ideas, *The Lunch Box* has come to the rescue!

# anatomy of a lunch box

Thanks to the rising popularity of bento-style lunch containers, your kid's midday meal can be nothing more involved than a varied little hodgepodge of foods. Just aim to make it a well-rounded hodgepodge: always combine a *protein* (think hard-boiled egg, tofu, chicken, or yogurt); a *fruit and/or vegetable* (such as grapes, cherry tomatoes, and carrot sticks); and an item rich in *complex carbohydrates* (try multigrain bread, whole-wheat pasta, or brown rice).

**keep your cool**
With an insulated lunch box and a chilled freezer gel pack (or frozen water bottle), perishable food can stay cold and safe to eat until lunchtime. If you are filling a thermos with a warm lunch, make sure you heat the food so that it's piping hot; run the thermos under hot water to warm it, too.

wraps, sandwiches,
or other filling foods
that will fuel
them up

snackable vegetables,
like baby carrots, small
broccoli florets, celery
sticks, or edamame

fruit that's easy to transport and eat

something crunchy to munch on, from popcorn to trail mix to crackers

an interactive element, like a dip, to keep them engaged

fruit juice, water, or milk to wash it all down

**a week of lunches**

**monday**
ham & cheese pinwheels (page 39), grapes, hummus with cucumber spears (page 80), cinnamon-sugar popcorn (page 90)

+

**tuesday**
deviled eggs (page 86), cheese & crackers, cooked edamame, halved strawberries

+

**wednesday**
turkey club (page 16), goldfish-shaped crackers, apple slices & celery sticks with nut butter

+

**thursday**
mini quiches (page 72), pineapple & mango skewers, mini rice cakes

+

**friday**
chili con carne (page 63), cheesy corn bread sticks (page 99), orange slices, yogurt-covered raisins

# stocking your kitchen

Here's a list of ingredients that appear in the recipes that follow, convenience items that will help you round out lunches in a snap, and packing supplies that will make your life a lot easier.

## pantry staples

- apples & bananas
- avocados & cherry tomatoes
- bread sticks & crackers
- canned refried beans
- canned tuna
- homemade or purchased pita chips or root veggie chips (page 81)
- homemade or purchased granola bars (page 93) or trail mix (page 94)
- nuts; raisins & other dried fruit
- precooked brown rice
- ramen noodles
- whole-grain bread & tortillas; mini pita breads; mini bagels
- whole-grain fig bars
- whole-grain pasta
- yogurt-covered raisins

## fridge & freezer staples

- grapes; berries; cherries; oranges & clementines
- presliced cheese, string cheese, mini Babybel cheese, baby mozzarella balls, goat cheese, cream cheese
- olives, dill pickles, cornichons
- hard-boiled eggs (page 105)
- jam; nut butter or tahini
- presliced deli meat
- precut vegetables
- yogurt & yogurt drinks
- homemade or purchased pesto (page 67), salsa (page 76), or hummus (page 80)
- frozen edamame, peas & corn
- frozen mini quiches (page 72), burritos (page 34), chili (page 63), or soup (page 60)

## packing supplies

- lunch box or bag (preferably insulated)
- aluminum foil, plastic wrap, wax paper
- gel cold packs
- thermos or other insulated container for warm meals
- plastic or metal food containers of varied sizes, including small ones for dips and salad dressings
- reusable water/juice bottle (freeze overnight to replace gel cold pack)
- sandwich bags (consider reusable or wax paper)
- sturdy bamboo or plastic utensils
- colorful silicone baking cups

Even a simple note lets your child know you're thinking about him when you're not together.

# marking a special day

Whether it's a holiday or special occasion or just an ordinary day, a few festive lunch box touches or a simple love note from you will raise spirits and bring a smile. No need to rush out to the craft store to buy supplies—just get creative with what you can find around the house.

## cute touches

**decorations**  Adorn containers, bags, or boxes with stickers or ribbons.

**labels**  Mark her lunch bag or a container with alphabet stamps or pens.

**enclosures**  Include a special note on a post-it, index card, strip of colorful wrapping paper, or even a photo.

**verses**  Compose a silly poem or song dedicated to your little one.

**jokes**  Write out a knock-knock joke or riddle from a kid's joke book on a slip of paper (fold in half to conceal the punch line).

**edible shapes**  Cut cheese or ham slices or sandwiches into shapes or letters with cookie or sandwich cutters.

**surprises**  Include a novelty gift: a glitter pen or rainbow pencil, a cute eraser, a sticker, a plastic toy, Silly Band(z), or other inexpensive trinkets.

## days to mark

**holidays**  Beyond the heavy hitters like Halloween and Valentine's, try getting creative with April Fool's Day, Groundhog Day, or other second-tier "holidays."

**birthdays**  If you're going to be so cruel as to send Junior to school on his birthday, at the very least, sneak a treat into his lunch box.

**test or game day**  Let your child know she's got someone in her corner when she's sweating over a school day challenge.

**tough days**  OK, so he flubbed the test or the game. Send him a note the next day to let him know you still think he's a star!

### dress it up

Make any day special with fun packaging ideas to spruce up the lunch box:

- colored or frilly toothpicks for berries
- cocktail umbrellas or decorative paper flags for sandwiches or cupcakes
- small bamboo skewers for cut fruit or pinwheels (pages 38–39)
- reusable straws, preferably those that bend or feature whimsical shapes
- take-out containers and chopsticks for Asian noodles (pages 54–55)

Presliced cheese will save you time on busy mornings.

Put leftover chicken breast to good use (page 25).

If their favorite combo is messy, wrap it in foil or wax paper so they can unwrap it as they go.

A spread, like hummus or mayo, acts as the "glue" to hold the sandwich together.

# the sandwich board

Take your sandwich game from good to great with the dozens
of ideas in the pages that follow. Or, get creative with what's
already in your fridge using this delicious road map as a guide.

## the foundation

sliced white, wheat, multigrain, rye, or sourdough bread; focaccia; French roll; hot dog
or hamburger bun; buttermilk biscuit; English muffin; croissant; bagel; pita pocket

## the fillings

### protein

hard-boiled egg, chopped
cooked chicken, canned tuna

+

### mix-ins

mayo, olive oil, lemon juice,
mustard, pickle relish, celery,
chopped fresh herbs

+

### add-ons

lettuce, tomato, sprouts,
cucumber

### meat & cheese

turkey, salami, pastrami,
roast beef, ham, bacon,
Cheddar, Swiss, Monterey jack,
provolone, havarti, mozzarella

+

### spread

mustard, mayo, hummus,
pesto, tapenade, cream cheese

+

### add-ons

lettuce, tomato, sprouts, onion,
avocado, cucumber, pickle

### savory spread

nut butter, cream cheese, goat
cheese, ricotta cheese

+

### sweet spread

fruit jam, honey, Nutella

+

### add-ons

banana slices, apple slices,
pear slices, strawberry slices,
pomegranate seeds

# classic turkey club

Lightly toast the bread. Spread 2 of the slices with the mayonnaise, and smash the avocado, if using, on top of the third slice. Fold the turkey slices to fit on top of the avocado-spread slice and sprinkle with salt and pepper. Place a slice on top of the turkey, mayonnaise side up. Pile on the lettuce leaves and tomato slices. Arrange the bacon slices on the tomatoes. Top with the remaining bread slice, mayonnaise side down. Press gently.

Insert 3 toothpicks deep into the layers, centering them on the sandwich in the shape of a triangle. Using a sharp knife, cut the sandwich around the toothpicks into 3 similar-sized pieces. Slip carefully into a sandwich bag, or arrange in a container, and seal tightly. Refrigerate until ready to go.

**whole-grain bread**  3 slices

**mayonnaise**  2 tablespoons

**ripe avocado**  3 slices (optional)

**roasted turkey breast**  3 slices

**salt and ground pepper**

**butter lettuce leaves**  2

**small tomato**  4 slices

**cooked bacon**  2 slices

**MAKES 1 LARGE SANDWICH**

## mix it up

• Try using other sliced deli meats, like roast beef, ham, or prosciutto, in place of turkey.

• To make a veggie club, omit the turkey and bacon, and add sliced cheese. Substitute hummus for the mayo.

• A fun serving idea: Omit the tomato slices from the sandwich. Cut the sandwich into squares and thread the sections onto a long skewer. Separate each square with a cherry tomato.

To avoid dreaded "soggy bread syndrome," pile the bacon on top of the tomato slices.

# gobblers

*irresistible sandwiches of all shapes and sizes*
*that won't come back uneaten*

## italian meat lover's

Spread mustard and mayo on the cut sides of a split hot dog bun or French roll. Add a layer of sliced provolone cheese. Follow with a layer of sliced ham and then a layer of sliced salami. Add black olives, pickles, and/or shredded lettuce, if you like.

## thanksgiving special

Spread a layer of cranberry relish on 2 slices of whole-wheat or sourdough bread. Between those slices, layer leftover roast turkey or sliced deli turkey, havarti or Cheddar cheese, and lettuce. If you have leftover stuffing or mashed potatoes, pile it on.

## parisian picnic

Cut a hunk of baguette into thin slices. Spread half of the slices with a layer of softened Brie cheese and the other half with a thin layer of Dijon mustard. Place a slice of ham on top of the cheese-covered slices, folding the ham to fit. Top with the remaining bread slices, mustard side down, and *voilà!* For a French-themed lunch box, include a small container of cornichons and niçoise olives.

## english teatime

In a small bowl, combine a few spoonfuls of softened cream cheese with a handful of chopped fresh basil. Spread 2 slices of whole-wheat or sourdough bread with a thin layer of the basil cream cheese. Top 1 slice with thin cucumber slices. Sprinkle with salt and pepper. Top with the remaining bread slice. Remove the crusts and cut the sandwich into small squares or triangles.

# philly cheesesteak roll

To make the "special sauce," in a small bowl, combine the mayonnaise, BBQ sauce, mustard, and onion. Season to taste with salt and pepper.

In a small frying pan, warm the olive oil over medium-high heat. Add the bell pepper and onion and cook until the vegetables are softened, about 3 minutes.

Preheat the broiler. Spread the sauce on the cut sides of the bun (or divide among the rolls). Place the bun bottom, cut side up, on a baking sheet. Add the steak, followed by the cheese and the pepper-onion mixture. Place under the broiler until the cheese melts, 1–2 minutes. Remove from the oven and replace the bun top. Wrap in foil, if you like, to help keep the sandwich warm. Slide into an insulated bag or container and seal tightly.

**FOR THE "SPECIAL SAUCE"**

**mayonnaise**  1 tablespoon

**BBQ sauce**  1 tablespoon

**grainy mustard**  1 teaspoon

**red onion**  1 tablespoon minced

**salt and ground pepper**

**olive oil**  1 teaspoon

**red or green bell pepper**  ¼, thinly sliced

**red onion**  ¼, thinly sliced

**hamburger bun**  1, or 2 small dinner rolls, split

**leftover cooked steak**  ½ cup (3 oz/90 g) sliced, or 2 slices roast beef

**provolone cheese**  2 thin slices

**MAKES 1 ROLL OR 2 MINI ROLLS**

## on a roll

**pulled pork**  Mix cooked, shredded pork or chicken with BBQ sauce and pile the mixture on the roll(s). Add shredded cabbage, if you like.

**five-spice tofu**  Use cooked, sliced tofu and grated carrot; make a sauce with mayo, fresh lime juice, five-spice powder, and fresh cilantro to taste.

Use leftover steak or deli-style roast beef for this kid-friendly version of a classic cheesesteak.

# egg salad on mini bagels

Put the eggs in a bowl. Using a fork, mash the eggs against the bottom and sides of the bowl until small chunks form. Toss with just enough mayonnaise to bind the eggs together, then add the mustard. Mix until blended and a little creamy. Season to taste with salt and pepper. Stir in the parsley, if using.

Lightly toast the bagels. Pile the egg salad onto the bagel bottoms and top with the cucumber slices. Cover with the bagel tops and press gently. (You will have some extra egg salad; use for additional sandwiches or as a snack with crackers later in the week.) Wrap each in foil and slip into a sandwich bag, or arrange in a container; seal tightly. Refrigerate until ready to go.

**hard-boiled eggs (page 105)**  2, peeled

**mayonnaise**  1–2 tablespoons

**yellow mustard**  1 teaspoon

**salt and ground pepper**

**fresh flat-leaf parsley**  1 tablespoon minced (optional)

**mini bagels**  2, split

**cucumber**  6 thin slices

**MAKES 2 MINI SANDWICHES**

## more mini-bagel ideas

**cream cheese classic**  Spread the halved, toasted bagels generously with whipped cream cheese or lox schmear. Stud with capers and layer with thinly sliced cucumber.

**pizza bagels**  Spread the halved bagels with pizza sauce; sprinkle with cheese and other toppings. Place under the broiler until the cheese melts, 2–3 minutes.

# tuna salad cutouts

In a bowl, combine the tuna, celery, parsley, lemon juice, pickle relish, if using, and just enough mayonnaise to bind it all together. Toss with a fork until well mixed. Pile the tuna mixture on 2 of the bread slices, dividing it evenly, and top with the remaining slices. Press gently. (You can also make 1 sandwich and save the extra tuna salad for a snack with crackers later in the week.)

Using a sandwich shape-cutter or a cookie cutter, press down firmly on the sandwiches to cut them into shapes. Discard (or snack on) the scraps. Wrap each in foil and slip into sandwich bags, or arrange in containers; seal tightly. Refrigerate until ready to go.

**water-packed white albacore tuna** 1 can (6 oz/185 g), drained

**celery or bell pepper** 2 tablespoons finely diced

**fresh flat-leaf parsley** 1 tablespoon minced

**fresh lemon juice** 2 teaspoons

**sweet pickle relish or chopped capers** 1 tablespoon (optional)

**mayonnaise** 1–2 tablespoons

**sourdough or white bread** 4 thin slices

**MAKES 2 SANDWICHES**

## fun with cutouts

Cookie cutters can be used to cut a sandwich into fun shapes that your kid will love. Try a heart on Valentine's Day, a four-leaf clover on St. Patrick's Day, or a snowman in December. Specialized sandwich cutters are also widely available, and make fewer scraps. Cutting the sandwich into multiple small, cute shapes allows kids to snack on the sandwiches throughout the day. Or, use alphabet cutters to spell your kid's initials in edible letters.

Here's a perfect Monday lunch to follow a Sunday roast chicken dinner.

# zesty chicken salad pita pockets

Cut a slice off the top of each mini pita and carefully pull apart at the cut side to make a pocket (or, if using a regular pita, cut it in half and pull each half apart at the cut side).

In a bowl, combine the yogurt, mustard, and lemon juice and mix until smooth. Add the chicken, apple, and celery and toss until the ingredients are evenly distributed. Season to taste with salt and pepper.

Line each pita pocket with a lettuce leaf, if using. (Lettuce is recommended to avoid a soggy pita.) Spoon the chicken salad inside, dividing it evenly. Wrap each snugly in foil and slip into a sandwich bag, or arrange in a container; seal tightly. Refrigerate until ready to go.

**pita bread** 3 mini rounds or one 6-inch (15-cm) round

**plain yogurt or mayonnaise** 2–3 tablespoons

**grainy or Dijon mustard** 1 teaspoon

**fresh lemon juice** 1 teaspoon

**cooked chicken** $3/4$ cup (4$1/2$ oz/140 g) cubed

**apple** $1/4$ cup (1 oz/30 g) diced

**celery** 2 tablespoons finely diced

**salt and ground pepper**

**butter lettuce** 2 leaves (optional)

**MAKES 3 MINI PITA POCKETS OR 2 LARGE PITA POCKETS**

## mix it up

- Add chopped fresh herbs like tarragon, dill, or parsley.
- Substitute diced fennel or jicama for the celery.
- Add toasted chopped walnuts or pecans.
- Omit the mustard and add $1/2$ teaspoon curry powder.
- Add diced ham or salami.
- For a vegetarian version, swap the chicken for chopped canned artichoke hearts.

# fruitwiches lunchtime eye candy featuring kids' favorite food group

### pear & avocado

Mash ½ ripe avocado in a bowl. Add a squeeze of fresh lemon juice and season to taste with salt and pepper. Spread the avocado evenly on 2 slices of bread. Add a layer of thinly sliced Bosc or Asian pear to one of the slices. Cover with the other slice and press gently to adhere. Swap in pomegranate seeds for the pear, if you like.

### strawberry & goat cheese

Split an English muffin and lightly toast the halves. Spread the cut side of the bottom half with softened goat cheese or plain whipped cream cheese. Top with a thin layer of strawberry jam, followed by a layer of thin strawberry slices. Cover with the top half of the muffin, jam side down, and press gently.

## oney, lmond utter & banana

Spread 2 slices of whole-wheat bread with almond butter or peanut butter. Top 1 bread slice with a drizzle of honey and a layer of banana slices. Cover with the other slice, butter side down, and press gently.

## apple, cheddar & peanut butter

Split a focaccia square in half crosswise. Spread the cut side of 1 half with peanut butter. Top with a layer of Cheddar cheese slices and then a layer of thin apple slices. Cover with the other half, cut side down, and press gently.

# wrap & roll

Need a break from the same old same old? Wraps are the perfect portable package, and kids just love them. You'll find a handful of great ideas in this chapter, or create your own using the guide below.

## the essentials

### the wrapper
tortilla (white, wheat, sun-dried tomato, spinach, or corn), lavash, chapati (Indian flatbread), nori (seaweed), romaine or red-leaf lettuce

### the "glue"
cream cheese, Brie cheese, goat cheese, hummus, mashed avocado, jam or chutney, pizza sauce, mayo, pesto, olive tapenade, refried beans

### the fillings
sliced deli meat, shredded chicken, smoked salmon, cooked bacon, tuna or egg salad, cheese, chopped salad, vegetables or fruit, rice, salsa

### wrap like a pro
1 Spread the wrapper with an even layer of your "glue." Add the filling ingredients in layers, or arrange them in a horizontal line across the center of the wrapper.

2 For a hand roll–style wrap, fold the right side of the wrapper over the filling, then roll up into a tight cylinder (the filling will peek out the other side). For a burrito-style wrap, fold the right and left sides over the filling before rolling (the filling will be enclosed).

### pack like an expert
Wrap in foil or wax paper and secure with a string or ribbon. To keep a cold wrap cool, pack next to an ice pack or chilled water bottle. To keep a heated wrap warm, place in the oven after it's wrapped in foil, and pack in an insulated bag or container away from any foods that should be kept cool. Thread pinwheels (page 38) on a skewer and pack them in an airtight container, or fit individual pinwheels snugly in an airtight container.

# fiesta veggie wrap

In a small bowl, mix together the cream cheese and pesto. Spread the cream cheese mixture evenly over the tortilla. Top with the avocado slices, arranging them in a horizontal line across the center or mashing them onto the surface. Arrange the carrot and cucumber on top of the avocado. Sprinkle with salt and pepper. Press down gently.

Fold about 2 inches (5 cm) of the right side of the tortilla over the filling. Press gently. Beginning with the rounded side closest to you, roll up the tortilla into a tight cylinder, with the filling peeking out the top. Alternatively, roll up the tortilla like you would a burrito, with the filling enclosed in the wrap (see page 34).

Wrap in foil or a strip of pretty paper and place in an airtight container or sandwich bag and seal tightly. Refrigerate until ready to go.

**cream cheese or goat cheese** 2 tablespoons, softened

**pesto, homemade (page 67) or purchased** 2 teaspoons

**flour tortilla** 1, preferably green or red

**ripe avocado** ½, sliced

**carrot** ¼ cup (1 oz/30 g) shredded

**English cucumber** 4 slices, cut on the diagonal

**salt and ground pepper**

**MAKES 1 WRAP**

## veggie-riffic

For extra color and crunch, add any of the following veggies:

- Celery or jicama matchsticks
- Sliced fennel
- Bell pepper matchsticks
- Baby spinach leaves
- Shredded red cabbage
- Sprouts

Use a napkin or colorful strip
of paper, secured with tape, to
hold the wrap together.

# rockin' wraps
Fun and flavor-packed handfuls that will be the star of the lunch table

## hummus & veggie wrap

Spread a flour tortilla or 2 corn tortillas with a thin layer of hummus, homemade (page 80) or purchased. Mash a couple of ripe avocado slices on top. Add baby spinach and red bell pepper strips in a horizontal line across the center. Roll up the tortilla into a tight cylinder, either hand-roll style or burrito style (see page 29).

## blt wrap

Spread a flour tortilla with a thin layer of mayo or softened cream cheese. Place 2 strips of cooked applewood-smoked bacon in a horizontal line across the center of the tortilla. Top the bacon with chopped romaine lettuce and chopped tomato. Roll up the tortilla into a tight cylinder, either hand-roll style or burrito style (see page 29).

## salad wrap

Prepare the Asian Chicken Salad (page 45), Chopped Caesar Salad (page 44), Greek Salad (page 46), or Creamy Waldorf Salad (page 48). Lay a flour tortilla on a work surface and spread the salad in a horizontal line across the center of the tortilla. Roll up the tortilla into a tight cylinder, either hand-roll style or burrito style (see page 29).

## pizza wrap

Spread a flour tortilla with a thin layer of pizza sauce or tomato paste. Sprinkle with shredded mozzarella cheese. Transfer to a baking sheet lined with foil and bake at 400°F (200°C) to melt the cheese, if you like. Add a few toppings, like salami, ham, mushrooms, or black olives. Roll up the tortilla into a tight cylinder, either hand-roll style or burrito style (see page 29).

# bean & cheese burrito

Preheat the oven to 400°F (200°C). Line a baking sheet with foil. Place the tortilla on the foil. Spread the beans in a horizontal line down the center of the tortilla and sprinkle with the cheese. Bake until the cheese melts and the beans are heated through, about 5 minutes.

Top the cheese with the salsa, avocado, and sour cream, if using. Fold about 2 inches (5 cm) of the left and right sides of the tortilla over the filling, and then roll up the tortilla into a tight cylinder. Wrap the burrito in the foil. Place in an insulated bag or container and seal tightly.

**flour tortilla** 1

**refried beans** ¼ cup (2 oz/60 g)

**Monterey jack or Colby cheese** 2 tablespoons shredded

**tomato salsa, homemade (page 76) or purchased** 1–2 tablespoons

**ripe avocado** 3 slices, or 2 tablespoons guacamole (page 79)

**sour cream** 1 tablespoon (optional)

**MAKES 1 BURRITO**

### freeze it!

If you want to use up the can of beans and have extra burritos on hand for future lunches, just quadruple this recipe to make 4 burritos (but hold off on adding the salsa, avocado, and sour cream until serving). Let the remaining burritos cool, then wrap in plastic wrap and place in a zippered plastic bag. Freeze for up to 3 months. Thaw overnight in the fridge, or reheat in the microwave.

# more burrito ideas

## steak & salsa verde

Add cooked, chopped steak or cooked ground beef along with the beans, and use green tomatillo salsa instead of tomato salsa.

## chicken & rice

Substitute black or pinto beans for the refried beans. Add cooked, shredded chicken and cooked rice for a hearty, full-meal burrito.

## super veggie

Add leftover cooked vegetables, chopped if necessary, along with the beans. If you don't have cooked vegetables on hand, sauté bell pepper strips and onion slices in olive oil until softened, about 3 minutes.

## burrito in a bowl

Substitute black or pinto beans for the refried beans, and substitute about ½ cup (2½ oz/75 g) cooked rice for the tortilla. Throw all the ingredients together in an insulated container.

**packing tips** For a special touch, write your child's name on the foil-wrapped burrito with a permanent marker, like they would at a takeout burrito shop. To keep the burrito warm for lunchtime, slide it into an adult-sized coffee thermos after heating it and wrapping it in foil.

Pack extra peanut dip on the side, along with some vegetable dippers, like cucumber spears.

# chicken & rice wrap with peanut dip

Preheat the oven to 400°F (200°C). Line a baking sheet with foil. Spread the 2 tablespoons peanut dip in a horizontal line across the center of the tortilla and top with the rice, chicken, spinach, and mandarin oranges. Fold about 2 inches (5 cm) of the left and right sides of the tortilla over the filling, and then roll up the tortilla into a tight cylinder.

Wrap in the foil and bake until all the ingredients are heated through, about 8 minutes. Slice the wrap in half crosswise, on the diagonal, through the foil, if you like, to expose the filling. Place in an insulated bag or container and seal tightly. Pack extra dip on the side.

**peanut-sesame dip (page 76)** 2 tablespoons, plus more for dipping

**whole-wheat flour tortilla** 1

**cooked brown rice (page 104)** 1/3 cup (1½ oz/45 g)

**cooked chicken** 1/3 cup (2 oz/60 g) shredded

**baby spinach** 1/4 cup (½ oz/15 g) chopped

**canned mandarin oranges** 1/4 cup (1½ oz/45 g), drained

**MAKES 1 WRAP**

## substitution, please!

**If meat is out of the question:** Substitute canned chickpeas, rinsed and drained, or cooked tofu for the chicken.

**If nuts are a no-no:** Use a bottled Asian sesame dressing, or even hummus (page 80), in place of the peanut-sesame dip.

**If oranges won't fly:** Swap in chopped red bell pepper or shredded red cabbage for color and crunch.

# pinwheels
## Colorful spirals created by slicing a wrap crosswise

### smoked salmon & cucumber

In a small bowl, mix together about 2 tablespoons softened cream cheese and some chopped fresh herbs. Spread the herbed cream cheese evenly over a flour tortilla or lavash sheet. Cover with a layer of thinly sliced smoked salmon. Draw a vegetable peeler along a peeled cucumber to create 6 thin slices. Arrange the slices over the salmon. Roll up the tortilla into a tight cylinder. Trim the ends, and then cut the cylinder crosswise into slices.

### salami & brie

Preheat the oven to 350°F (180°C). Place a flour tortilla on a baking sheet and dot it with small pieces of Brie. Bake until the cheese melts, about 5 minutes. Spread the melted cheese in an even layer, and then cover the cheese with a layer of salami slices. Roll up the tortilla into a tight cylinder. Trim the ends, and then cut the cylinder crosswise into slices. Make it meatless by substituting olive tapenade for the salami.

To help them hold their shape, thread pinwheels on skewers or toothpicks. Snip off the pointy tips.

### turkey, cheese & salsa

Preheat the oven to 350°F (180°C). Place a flour tortilla on a baking sheet and sprinkle shredded Monterey jack cheese over the top. Bake until the cheese melts, about 5 minutes. Arrange turkey slices over the cheese, and then top with a few spoonfuls of salsa and/or mashed avocado. Roll up the tortilla into a tight cylinder. Trim the ends, and then cut the cylinder crosswise into slices.

### ham & cheese

Spread a flour tortilla with a thin layer of mayo, followed by a thin layer of grainy mustard. Add a layer of sliced ham and then sprinkle with shredded Cheddar cheese. Transfer to a baking sheet and bake at 350°F (180°C) to melt the cheese, if you like. Roll up the tortilla into a tight cylinder. Trim the ends, and then cut the cylinder crosswise into slices.

# veggie sushi rolls

Place the rice in a microwave-safe bowl. Add a few drops of water and microwave on high until the rice is warm and softened, about 30 seconds. Set the rice aside to cool.

In a small bowl, combine the vinegar with 2 tablespoons water. Place a bamboo sushi mat on a work surface with the bamboo strips facing you horizontally. Place the nori sheet horizontally, shiny side down, on the mat, aligned with the edge nearest you. Dip your hands into the vinegar-water mixture and spread the cooled rice in an even layer over the nori sheet, leaving the top one-fourth of the nori uncovered. Sprinkle the sesame seeds over the rice, then arrange the cucumber and carrot sticks and the avocado slices in a horizontal strip across the bottom portion of the rice.

Starting at the edge closest to you, lift the mat, nori, and rice over the filling to seal it inside, then roll up the sushi into a tight cylinder. Use your finger to lightly moisten the outer edge of the nori with the vinegar-water mixture to seal the roll. Dipping a sharp knife in water before each cut, cut the roll in half crosswise, and then cut each half crosswise into 4 equal pieces.

Pack the sushi snugly into an airtight container and sprinkle with sesame seeds. Refrigerate until ready to go. Include little containers of soy sauce and/or pickled ginger, if you like. And don't forget the chopsticks!

**cooked sushi rice (page 104)**
1¼ cups (6 oz/185 g)

**unseasoned rice vinegar**  1 teaspoon

**toasted nori seaweed**  1 sheet, about 7 by 8 inches (18 by 20 cm)

**toasted sesame seeds**  1 tablespoon, plus more for sprinkling

**English cucumber**  ¼, peeled and cut into thin matchsticks

**carrot**  ½, peeled and cut into thin matchsticks

**ripe avocado**  ¼, thinly sliced

**soy sauce and pickled ginger slices** for serving (optional)

**MAKES 1 SUSHI ROLL (8 PIECES)**

Create "training chopsticks" by binding the top ends together and then wedging them apart.

# the salad bar

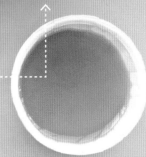

Salads are more kid-friendly than you might think—they can be easily tailored to suit your child's ever-changing food preferences.

# chopped caesar salad

Put the lettuce in a container with a tight-fitting lid and add the salad dressing. Cover the container tightly and toss gently until the lettuce is evenly coated with the dressing.

Uncover and top with the chicken, if using. Using a vegetable peeler, shave thin pieces from the wedge of cheese over the salad. Sprinkle with pepper to taste. Cover and refrigerate until ready to go.

Pack in a portable lunch cooler, if you have one, to keep the salad cool. Place the croutons in a small container or bag and pack along with the salad. Don't forget to pack a fork!

**romaine lettuce**  1½ cups
(1½ oz/45 g) roughly chopped

**Caesar salad dressing, homemade (see note) or purchased**  about 2 tablespoons

**cooked chicken**  ½ cup (3 oz/90 g) sliced or shredded (optional)

**Parmesan cheese**  small wedge

**ground pepper**

**prepared croutons**  ¼ cup (⅓ oz/10 g)

**MAKES 1 SERVING**

### caesar salad dressing

In a blender, combine 1 tablespoon mayonnaise; 1 garlic clove, chopped; 1–3 anchovy fillets, chopped (optional); 2 teaspoons Dijon mustard; the juice from 1 lemon; 1 teaspoon Worcestershire sauce; ¼ cup (2 fl oz/60 ml) olive oil; 1 teaspoon salt; and a few grindings of pepper. Blend until smooth. Makes about ½ cup (4 fl oz/125 ml) dressing. Transfer any remaining dressing to a jar, close tightly, and store in the fridge for up to 5 days.

# asian chicken salad

In a container with a tight-fitting lid, combine the salad greens, cucumber, snow peas, chicken, almonds, and mandarin oranges. Cover the container tightly and toss gently until the ingredients are evenly distributed. Cover and refrigerate until ready to go.

Pack in a portable lunch cooler, if you have one, to keep the salad cool. Pour the dressing into a small container and pack it along with the salad. Don't forget to pack a fork!

**mixed baby greens or thinly shredded green cabbage** 1 cup (1 oz/30 g)

**English cucumber** 2-inch (5-cm) piece, quartered lengthwise and sliced crosswise

**snow peas** 4–6, trimmed and halved

**cooked chicken** ½ cup (3 oz/90 g) shredded

**toasted sliced almonds** 1 tablespoon

**canned mandarin oranges** ¼ cup (1½ oz/45 g), drained

**Asian-style salad dressing, homemade (see note) or purchased** about 2 tablespoons

**MAKES 1 SERVING**

## asian-style salad dressing

In a jar, combine 2 tablespoons teriyaki sauce, 1 tablespoon canola oil, 1 tablespoon mayonnaise, 1 tablespoon rice vinegar, 1 teaspoon sesame oil, and 1 teaspoon peeled, grated fresh ginger. Close tightly and shake to mix well. Makes about ⅓ cup (3 fl oz/80 ml) dressing. Store any remaining dressing in the fridge for up to 5 days.

# greek salad

In a jar or other small container with a lid, combine the olive oil, vinegar, and a generous amount of pepper. Cover and shake to combine. Pack the pita chips in a small container or bag.

In a container with a tight-fitting lid, combine the lettuce, cucumber, tomatoes, onion, olives, and cheese. Cover the container tightly and toss gently until the ingredients are evenly distributed. Refrigerate until ready to go.

Pack the salad in a portable lunch cooler, if you have one, to keep it cool. Pack the pita chips and the dressing along with the salad to be sprinkled on top before eating. Don't forget to pack a fork!

**olive oil** 1½ tablespoons

**red wine vinegar** 2 teaspoons

**ground pepper**

**pita chips, homemade (page 81) or purchased**

**romaine lettuce** 1 cup (1 oz/30 g) roughly chopped

**English cucumber** 2-inch (5-cm) piece, quartered lengthwise and sliced crosswise

**cherry tomatoes** ¼ cup (1½ oz/45 g) halved

**red onion** 1 tablespoon chopped

**pitted Kalamata or other olives** 2 tablespoons chopped

**feta cheese** 2 tablespoons crumbled

**MAKES 1 SERVING**

## sell it!

Make any salad more appealing by including a crunchy component, like pita chips, for sprinkling over the salad. Other possibilities include croutons, toasted oil-brushed baguette rounds, or pine nuts.

Nestle the dressing container in the salad container to avoid spills and make it easy to find.

# creamy waldorf salad

In a bowl, toss the apple with the lemon juice. Add the celery, chives, and nuts. In another bowl, combine the sour cream, mustard, and honey. Whisk together until blended. Season to taste with salt and pepper. Add the dressing to the apple mixture and stir to mix well.

Place the lettuce in a container with a tight-fitting lid and spoon the apple mixture on top. Cover tightly and refrigerate until ready to go.

Pack in a portable lunch cooler, if you have one, to keep the salad cool. Don't forget to pack a fork!

**apple** ½ cup (2 oz/60 g) diced

**fresh lemon juice** from ¼ lemon

**celery** ⅓ cup (1½ oz/45 g) diced

**fresh chives** 1 teaspoon minced

**walnut or pecan halves** ¼ cup (1 oz/30 g), toasted and chopped

**sour cream or plain yogurt** 2 tablespoons

**Dijon mustard** ½ teaspoon

**honey** ½ teaspoon

**salt and ground pepper**

**butter lettuce** 1 small head, inner leaves only, torn

**MAKES 1 SERVING**

## substitution, please!

**If creamy stuff isn't their favorite:** Omit the sour cream, mustard, and honey and use a simple salad dressing, like balsamic vinaigrette, instead.

**If green stuff doesn't float their boat:** Omit the celery, chives, and lettuce. Serve the salad with sturdy crackers or stuff it into mini pita pockets.

# make-your-own taco salad

In a jar or other small container with a lid, stir together the salsa and sour cream to make a dressing. In another small container or a bag, combine the cheese and crumbled tortilla chips.

In a container with a tight-fitting lid, combine the lettuce, tomatoes, beans, and olives. Cover the container and shake to combine the ingredients. Refrigerate until ready to go.

Pack in a portable lunch cooler, if you have one, to keep the salad cool. Pack the salsa dressing and cheesy chip topping along with the salad; include a note reminding your child to assemble the salad before eating. Don't forget to pack a fork! For a bigger appetite, pack a tortilla with the salad for making a taco salad wrap.

**tomato salsa, homemade (page 76) or purchased** 2 tablespoons

**sour cream** 1 tablespoon

**Monterey jack cheese** 1/4 cup (1 oz/30 g) shredded

**tortilla chips** 1/3 cup (1 oz/30 g) crumbled

**lettuce** 1 1/2 cups (1 1/2 oz/45 g) shredded

**tomatoes** 1/4 cup (1 1/2 oz/45 g) chopped

**canned black, kidney, or pinto beans** 1/4 cup (2 oz/60 g), rinsed and drained

**black olives** 2 tablespoons sliced

**flour tortilla** 1 (optional)

**MAKES 1 SERVING**

### leftover special

This is a great salad to pack for lunch the day after a family taco dinner. If you have any leftover taco meat, add that to the salad as well.

# orzo & grilled veggie salad

In a bowl, whisk together the olive oil and lemon juice. Season to taste with salt and pepper. Add the orzo and stir to combine.

Put half of the orzo in a container with a tight-fitting lid. Add half of the vegetables. Layer the remaining orzo on top, followed by the remaining vegetables. Sprinkle with the cheese and the basil, if using. Cover tightly and refrigerate until ready to go. Don't forget to pack a fork!

**olive oil**  2 tablespoons

**fresh lemon juice**  1 tablespoon

**salt and ground pepper**

**cooked orzo or other small pasta shapes**  1 cup (6 oz/185 g)

**leftover grilled vegetables such as zucchini, eggplant, bell peppers, or mushrooms**  ½–1 cup (3–6 oz/90–185 g) chopped

**crumbled feta or grated Parmesan cheese**  2 tablespoons

**fresh basil**  1 tablespoon thinly shredded (optional)

**MAKES 1 SERVING**

## mix it up

In place of the grilled vegetables, try swapping in:

- Cooked, chopped artichoke hearts (you can find them frozen or canned) and chopped sun-dried tomatoes
- Cooked broccoli florets and sliced almonds or toasted pine nuts
- Thawed frozen vegetables mixed with a little bit of pesto (page 67)
- Baby mozzarella balls and halved cherry tomatoes

# stealth side salads

chunky salads perfect for youngsters who have vowed
never to let a shred of lettuce pass their lips

## tuna & white bean

In a small container with
a tight-fitting lid, combine
2 teaspoons olive oil, 1 teaspoon
lemon juice, and ½ teaspoon
Dijon mustard. Add equal parts
canned white beans, rinsed
and drained, and canned tuna,
drained and flaked. Sprinkle
with minced celery and onion.
Cover and shake to combine.
Season with salt and pepper.

## corn & edamame

In a small container with
a tight-fitting lid, combine
2 teaspoons fresh lime juice
and 1 teaspoon olive oil. Add
equal parts cooked corn kernels;
cooked, shelled edamame;
halved cherry tomatoes; and
avocado cubes. Sprinkle with
minced cilantro, if you like.
Cover and shake to combine.
Season with salt and pepper.

## beet & feta

In a small container with
a tight-fitting lid, combine
1 tablespoon *each* olive oil and
orange juice and 1 teaspoon
balsamic vinegar. Peel and cube
2 roasted beets. Add to the
container, cover, and shake.
Add shredded carrot along
with (or in place of) the beets.
Sprinkle with feta cheese and
season with salt and pepper.

## orange & celery

In a small container with
a tight-fitting lid, combine
equal parts sliced or shaved
celery and seedless orange
segments. Drizzle with
1 tablespoon olive oil and
1 teaspoon white wine vinegar.
Cover and shake gently to
combine. Season with salt and
pepper. Sprinkle with chopped
fresh parsley, if you like.

Any of these would be
a great addition to a
bento-style lunch.

# peanut butter noodles with snow peas

Place the spaghetti in a container with a tight-fitting lid and add the peanut dip. Cover tightly and shake until the noodles are evenly coated. Uncover and add more dip, if needed.

Add the bell pepper strips, snow peas, green onion, and sesame seeds. Cover and shake again to combine. Refrigerate until ready to go. Pack chopsticks or a fork along with the salad.

**cooked spaghetti**  1 cup (6 oz/185 g)

**peanut-sesame dip (page 76)**  about 2 tablespoons

**red bell pepper**  ¼, sliced into thin strips

**snow peas**  ¼ cup (¾ oz/20 g), trimmed and halved

**green onion**  1, thinly sliced

**toasted sesame seeds**  1 teaspoon

**MAKES 1 SERVING**

## mix it up

To make this a more substantial meal, add cooked, shredded chicken; cooked, sliced sausages; or cooked, cubed tofu.

# crunchy ramen noodle salad

In a small saucepan, combine the olive oil, sugar, and vinegar and bring to a boil over medium-high heat. Stir to dissolve the sugar, remove from the heat, and let cool.

In a frying pan, melt the butter over medium heat. Add the ramen noodles, almonds, and sesame seeds and cook, stirring often, until light brown, about 4 minutes. Remove from the heat and let cool.

Place the cabbage and carrots in a large bowl and add the ramen noodle mixture. Pour the vinegar mixture over the top and toss until combined. Season to taste with salt and pepper.

Spoon the salad into an airtight container. Cover tightly and refrigerate until ready to go. Pack chopsticks or a fork along with the salad. (This salad is best eaten the same day, so pack the second portion for yourself or another family member.)

**olive oil** ¼ cup (2 fl oz/60 ml)

**sugar** 2 tablespoons

**apple cider vinegar** ⅓ cup (3 fl oz/80 ml)

**butter** 1 tablespoon

**ramen noodles** 1 package (3 oz/90 g), broken up (discard flavor packet)

**sliced almonds** ¼ cup (1 oz/30 g)

**sesame seeds** 2 tablespoons

**purple cabbage** 1½ cups (4½ oz/140 g) shredded

**carrots** 1½ cups (7½ oz/235 g) shredded

**salt and ground pepper**

**MAKES 2 SERVINGS**

## sell it!

Pack noodle salads in Chinese-style takeout containers stamped with your child's initials. Write out a fortune on a tiny piece of paper and bury it in a bag of popcorn or trail mix.

Turn leftover rice or pasta into a full meal by sneaking in veggies and protein.

Freeze soup in individual portions and defrost as needed for quick lunches.

Label containers with a marker or stickers to help avoid lunch-table mixups.

# warm & hearty

On those deepest, darkest days of the school year, packing a warm lunch sends your little one into the world with an extra touch of hominess and comfort.

Build a reserve of travel-ready forks, spoons, sporks, and other utensils.

No one likes cold oatmeal, so be sure to use a well-insulated container.

# oatmeal with toppings galore

In a heavy saucepan, bring the milk and a pinch of salt to a simmer over medium-high heat. Slowly stir in the oats. Reduce the heat to medium and cook at a gentle boil, uncovered, stirring often, until the oatmeal is soft and the milk is absorbed, about 5 minutes. Remove from the heat, cover, and let stand for 3 minutes.

Transfer to an insulated container. Top with a splash of cream and a sprinkle of brown sugar. Add other toppings, if you like (see below for some ideas). Close tightly to keep warm. Don't forget to pack a spoon!

**milk or water**  1 cup (8 fl oz/250 ml)

**salt**

**rolled oats**  1/2 cup (1 1/2 oz/45 g)

**heavy cream and brown sugar** for topping

**MAKES 1 SERVING**

## toppings to try

Oatmeal is a hearty base for just about any topping or stir-in you can think of. Here are some favorites:

- Top with fresh fruit, such as blueberries, raspberries, sliced strawberries, chopped peaches or nectarines, or chopped apples or pears.
- Sprinkle with cinnamon sugar and top with banana slices.
- Top with dried fruit and/or nuts and a drizzle of honey.
- Swirl in some fruit jam, applesauce, or honey.

# chicken & rice soup

Combine the broth, rice, and 2 cups (16 fl oz/500 ml) water in a saucepan. Place over medium heat and bring to a boil. Add the chicken to the saucepan and reduce the heat to low. Simmer the chicken, uncovered, until cooked through, 10–12 minutes. Using tongs, lift the chicken pieces out of the broth and put them on a plate. Set aside to cool.

Stir the carrot, celery, peas, garlic, and thyme into the saucepan. Raise the heat to medium and cook until the vegetables are softened and the rice is tender but not mushy, about 10 minutes. Taste the broth and season with salt and pepper to taste and a squeeze or two of lemon juice, if using.

Shred the chicken or cut it into bite-sized pieces and add it back to the simmering soup. Cook until heated through, about 5 minutes.

Ladle servings of the soup into insulated containers as needed and close tightly to keep warm. Don't forget to pack a spoon! (Let any remaining soup cool, then cover tightly and refrigerate for up to 4 days or freeze in individual portions for up to 4 months.)

**low-sodium chicken broth**  4 cups (32 fl oz/1 l)

**long-grain white rice**  1/3 cup (2 1/2 oz/75 g)

**skinless, boneless chicken breast halves**  2

**carrot**  1, peeled and diced

**celery**  1 stalk, diced

**frozen peas**  1 cup (5 oz/155 g)

**garlic**  1 clove, sliced

**thyme, dill, or parsley**  1/2 teaspoon dried or 1 teaspoon minced fresh

**salt and ground pepper**

**fresh lemon juice**  (optional)

**MAKES 4 SERVINGS**

## make it meatless

Omit the chicken and substitute vegetable broth for the chicken broth. Throw in some more vegetables, if you like, such as tomatoes, mushrooms, zucchini, corn, baby spinach, or asparagus. You can also swap out the rice for fun pasta shapes.

Pack crunchy crackers or pita chips
for crumbling or dipping.

Serve with corn bread sticks
(page 99) and fruit skewers.

# chili con carne

-----------------------------------------------------------------

In a large, heavy pot, warm the olive oil over medium heat. Add the onion and cook, stirring often, until translucent, about 5 minutes. Add the ground beef and garlic and cook, using a wooden spoon to break up the meat into small pieces, until the beef is browned, 5–7 minutes.

Add the chili powder, cumin, and oregano. Stir to mix well. Stir in the chicken broth, tomatoes and their juices, beans, and tomato paste and bring to a simmer. Reduce the heat to medium-low and cook until slightly thickened, 20–25 minutes. Season to taste with salt and pepper.

Spoon servings of the chili into insulated containers as needed and sprinkle a little cheese over the top of each. Close tightly to keep warm. Don't forget to pack a spoon! (Let any remaining chili cool, then cover tightly and refrigerate for up to 5 days or freeze in individual portions for up to 4 months.)

**olive oil**  1 tablespoon

**yellow onion**  ½ cup (2½ oz/75 g) chopped

**ground beef or turkey**  1 lb (500 g)

**garlic**  2 cloves, minced

**chili powder**  1–2 tablespoons

**ground cumin**  1 teaspoon

**dried oregano**  ½ teaspoon

**low-sodium chicken broth**  2 cups (16 fl oz/500 ml)

**crushed tomatoes**  1 can (14 oz/440 g)

**kidney, black, or pinto beans**  1 can (15 oz/470 g), rinsed and drained

**tomato paste**  2 tablespoons

**salt and ground pepper**

**Cheddar cheese**  ½ cup (2 oz/60 g) shredded

**MAKES 4 SERVINGS**

## top it off

Other yummy toppings for this hearty chili include sour cream, crumbled tortilla chips, chopped onion, and salsa.

# mac & cheese, all dressed up

Prepare the macaroni and cheese sauce according to the package directions. Stir in the extra cheeses and the vegetables. Cook gently over low heat until the cheese is melted and the vegetables are heated through, about 5 minutes.

Spoon servings into insulated containers as needed and close tightly to keep warm. Don't forget to pack a fork! (Let any remaining pasta cool, then cover tightly and refrigerate for up to 5 days.)

**all-natural macaroni and cheese** 1 package (6 oz/185 g)

**Cheddar, Monterey jack, or havarti cheese** ½ cup (2 oz/60 g) shredded

**Parmesan cheese** 2 tablespoons grated

**frozen vegetables such as peas, carrots, shelled edamame, and/or broccoli florets** 1 cup (5 oz/155 g)

**MAKES 2-4 SERVINGS**

## freeze it!

You can freeze leftover mac and cheese in individual portions for another day. To rewarm, sprinkle with a teaspoon of milk and then pop in the microwave. This helps bring back the creaminess.

# more ways to dress up mac & cheese

## chicken florentine

In a frying pan, heat
1 teaspoon olive oil over
medium heat. Add 1 cup
(2 oz/60 g) chopped spinach
and 1 cup (6 oz/185 g)
cooked, shredded chicken
and stir until the spinach
is wilted, 2–3 minutes. Stir
into the prepared mac
and cheese.

## tex mex

Add ½ cup (2 oz/60 g)
shredded pepper jack
cheese, ¼ cup (1½ oz/45 g)
chopped bell pepper, and
¼ cup (1½ oz/45 g) diced
canned tomatoes to the
prepared mac and cheese
and stir until the vegetables
are heated through, about
5 minutes.

## bacon & onion

Just before serving, sprinkle
the prepared mac and
cheese with 2 or 3 slices
cooked bacon, crumbled,
and 2 green onions, chopped.

## ham & cheese

Add 2 oz (60 g) diced ham
and ½ teaspoon grainy
mustard to the prepared
mac and cheese. Stir until
combined and the ham is
heated through, about
5 minutes.

Substitute any frozen veggies
that your kid is willing to eat.

# wagon wheels with pesto & broccoli

Bring a large pot of water to a boil over high heat. Stir in 1 tablespoon salt. Add the broccoli to the boiling water and cook until tender-crisp, about 2 minutes. Scoop out the broccoli, drain, and set aside.

Add the pasta to the boiling water. Cook, stirring occasionally to prevent sticking, until al dente, according to the package directions. Drain the pasta and transfer to a bowl. Add the pesto and stir to combine. Stir in the cooked broccoli and tomatoes and sprinkle with the Parmesan cheese. Add more pesto as needed to coat the tomatoes and broccoli.

Spoon servings of the pasta into insulated containers as needed and close tightly to keep warm. Don't forget to pack a fork! (Let any remaining pasta cool, then cover tightly and refrigerate for up to 4 days.)

salt

**small broccoli florets** 1 cup (2 oz/60 g)

**wagon wheel or other medium-sized pasta shape** 1 cup (3½ oz/105 g)

**pesto, homemade (see note) or purchased** about 3 tablespoons

**cherry tomatoes** 4–6, halved

**Parmesan cheese** 2 tablespoons grated

**MAKES 1 OR 2 SERVINGS**

### easy pesto

In a blender or food processor, combine 1 cup (1 oz/30 g) tightly packed basil leaves; 1 clove garlic; ¼ cup (2 fl oz/60 ml) olive oil; 2 tablespoons pine nuts; ¼ teaspoon salt; and several grindings of pepper. Process until a coarse paste forms. Transfer the pesto to a bowl and stir in ⅓ cup (1½ oz/45 g) grated Parmesan cheese. Makes about 1 cup (8 fl oz/250 ml). Leftover pesto can be stored in an airtight container in the fridge for up to 2 days or in the freezer for up to 2 months.

# teriyaki rice bowl

In a frying pan, heat the teriyaki sauce, hoisin sauce, and ginger over medium heat, stirring occasionally, until hot and bubbly, 2–3 minutes. Stir in the chicken and cook until heated through, about 5 minutes.

Meanwhile, bring a pot of water to a boil over high heat. Add the carrot and cook for 1 minute. Add the asparagus and cook for 1 minute more. Drain. Add the cooked, drained vegetables and the bell pepper strips to the pan with the chicken and stir to combine.

Place the rice in an insulated container. Pour the contents of the pan over the rice. Sprinkle with the sesame seeds. Close tightly to keep warm. Don't forget to pack a fork or chopsticks!

**teriyaki sauce** 3 tablespoons

**hoisin sauce** 1 teaspoon

**ginger** ¼ teaspoon grated fresh or ⅛ teaspoon ground

**cooked chicken** ½ cup (3 oz/90 g) cubed

**carrot** ½, peeled and cut into thin matchsticks

**thin asparagus spears** 3, woody ends removed, cut on the diagonal into 1-inch (2.5-cm) pieces

**red bell pepper** ¼ cup (1½ oz/45 g) thinly sliced

**cooked brown rice (page 104)** 1 cup (5 oz/155 g), warm

**toasted sesame seeds** 2 teaspoons

**MAKES 1 SERVING**

## mix it up

Just about any protein can stand in for the chicken. Try your child's favorite, such as cooked, cubed tofu or cooked and thinly sliced pork tenderloin or steak. Or, simply omit the meat for a veggie rice bowl.

# oh-so-simple fried rice

In a nonstick frying pan, warm 1 teaspoon of the peanut oil over medium-high heat. When the oil is hot, add the egg and swirl to make a thin pancake. As it sets, lift the edges of the pancake, tilting the pan to allow any uncooked egg to run underneath. When the pancake is set, transfer to a bowl. Let cool for a minute or so, then chop coarsely.

Wipe out the frying pan with a paper towel and return to medium-high heat. Add the remaining 4 teaspoons peanut oil. When the oil is hot, add the snow peas. Add a few drops of water to create steam, then toss and stir until the peas are slightly softened, 2–3 minutes. Add the rice and toss and stir until hot throughout, about 3 minutes, separating the grains with a spatula or wooden spoon. Add the ham, cooked egg, and green onions and toss and stir for about 30 seconds longer.

Remove from the heat. Season to taste with salt and pepper. Drizzle the sesame oil over the fried rice and toss a few times to blend. Spoon servings into insulated containers as needed and close tightly to keep warm. Don't forget to pack a fork! (Let any remaining rice cool, then cover tightly and refrigerate for up to 4 days.)

**peanut oil**  5 teaspoons

**large egg**  1, lightly beaten

**snow peas**  1 cup (4 oz/125 g), trimmed and halved, or 1 cup (5 oz/155 g) frozen vegetable medley

**cooked white rice (page 104)**  2 cups (10 oz/315 g), cold

**cooked ham**  2 oz (60 g), diced

**green onions**  2, thinly sliced on the diagonal

**salt and ground pepper**

**Asian sesame oil**  1 teaspoon

**MAKES 2 SERVINGS**

## what else?

Serve the rice with vegetable pot stickers (there are tons of great frozen options available) and cubed watermelon or mango.

# spinach & sausage frittata sticks

Let the package of spinach thaw slightly, then remove about one-fourth of the leaves. Reserve the remaining spinach for another use. Rinse the spinach in your hands over the sink and squeeze out any excess water.

In a frying pan, heat the oil over medium heat. Add the onion and cook, stirring often, until translucent, 3–4 minutes. Add the sausages and cook, stirring often and breaking up the meat, until brown and cooked through, 5–7 minutes. Remove from the heat and set aside.

Preheat the oven to 350°F (180°C) and butter an 8-inch (20-cm) square baking dish. Crack the eggs into a large bowl. Add the cream and whisk until blended. Add the cheese, spinach, and onion-sausage mixture. Stir gently until well blended.

Pour the egg mixture into the prepared dish. Bake the frittata until the eggs are golden and set, about 35 minutes. Transfer to a wire rack and let cool for a few minutes. Using a butter knife, loosen the frittata from the edges of the dish. Hold a large plate upside down over the dish, then turn the dish and plate together, releasing the frittata onto the plate. Cut the frittata into finger-sized sticks. Place in insulated containers to keep warm, or let cool and pack in sandwich bags. (Let any remaining frittata sticks cool, then place individual portions in zippered plastic bags and refrigerate for up to 4 days or freeze for up to 3 months.)

**frozen spinach leaves**  1 package (10 oz/315 g)

**olive oil**  1 tablespoon

**yellow onion**  1/4 cup (1 1/2 oz/45 g) chopped

**mild Italian sausages**  2, casings removed, broken into 1-inch (2.5-cm) pieces

**butter**  for greasing

**large eggs**  8

**heavy cream**  2 tablespoons

**Monterey jack cheese**  3/4 cup (3 oz/90 g) shredded

**MAKES 4–6 SERVINGS**

# ham & cheese mini quiches

Place the dough on a lightly floured surface and roll out until ⅛ inch (3 mm) thick. Using a 2½-inch (6-cm) biscuit cutter, cut out as many rounds as possible. Ease the rounds gently into the cups of a mini muffin pan. The edges of the dough should be flush with the rim of the pan. (You should have enough dough to line 12–16 cups. If needed, gather the scraps, roll out ⅛ inch thick, and cut out additional rounds.)

Preheat the oven to 400°F (200°C). In a large measuring cup, whisk together the eggs, cream, mustard, ¼ teaspoon salt, and a pinch of pepper. Divide the ham and bell pepper evenly among the lined cups, and then pour the egg mixture into the cups, dividing it evenly. Sprinkle the cheese evenly on top of the cups.

Bake until the quiches are puffy and golden brown, 18–20 minutes. Let cool in the pan on a wire rack for about 10 minutes. Run a knife around the sides of each cup and carefully lift out the quiches. If desired, place them in decorative paper baking cups. Pack into airtight containers and seal tightly. Refrigerate for up to 3 days.

**prepared pie dough or puff pastry dough**  1 sheet, thawed

**large eggs**  2

**heavy cream**  2 tablespoons

**Dijon mustard**  ½ teaspoon

**salt and ground pepper**

**ham**  1 oz (30 g), finely diced

**green or red bell pepper**  2 tablespoons finely diced

**Gruyère or Swiss cheese**  1 oz (30 g), finely grated

**MAKES 12–16 MINI QUICHES**

## freeze it!

Freeze remaining mini quiches to use for future lunches or afternoon snacks. Cool the quiches completely, wrap in plastic wrap or foil, and place in a zippered plastic bag. Freeze for up to 3 months. Reheat frozen quiches in the microwave on high for 25–35 seconds.

# dips & dippers

Pack salsa with tortilla chips, broccoli, mushrooms, or bell pepper.

Pack hummus with pita chips, cucumber, bell pepper, broccoli, carrots, or celery.

Pack tzatziki with crackers, carrots, celery, bell pepper, or cherry tomatoes.

Pack nut butter with pretzels, apple slices, or celery.

# cool dips

*make-ahead dips that are delicious,
diverse, and remarkably versatile*

- - - - - - - - - - - - - - - - - - - - - - - - - - - - - - - - - - - - - - - - - - -

### peanut-sesame dip

In a bowl, combine 1 tablespoon soy sauce, 2 teaspoons *each* sesame oil and rice vinegar, and 3 tablespoons creamy peanut butter. Whisk in 1–2 tablespoons hot water. Sprinkle with toasted sesame seeds, if you like. Makes about ½ cup (4 fl oz/125 ml).

### creamy herb dip

In a blender, combine ½ cup (4 oz/125 g) *each* plain yogurt and cottage cheese; 2 green onions, chopped; 2 teaspoons chopped fresh dill; a handful of fresh flat-leaf parsley; and ¼ teaspoon celery salt. Blend until smooth. Makes about 1 cup (8 oz/250 g).

### cucumber tzatziki

In a bowl, mix together 1 container (7 oz/220 g) plain yogurt; 1 cup (5 oz/155 g) peeled and grated or finely diced English cucumber; 1 teaspoon minced fresh mint or flat-leaf parsley; and a squeeze of lemon juice. Season to taste with salt. Makes about 2 cups (16 oz/500 g).

### chunky tomato salsa

In a bowl, mix together 1 can (14 oz/440 g) diced tomatoes with their juice (or 2 large, ripe tomatoes, chopped); ¼ cup (2 oz/60 g) chopped onion; 1 clove garlic, minced; and a handful of chopped fresh cilantro, if you like. Season to taste with lime juice, salt, and pepper. Add minced jalapeño chile, if you like. Makes about 2 cups (16 fl oz/500 ml).

Dippers they'll love: vegetable spears, chicken strips, crackers, sturdy chips, and breadsticks.

For easy dipping, use a clear,
wide-mouthed container that's
not too deep.

# mexican layer dip

-----

To make the guacamole, in a bowl, mash the avocado with the lime juice and cumin. Season to taste with salt and pepper.

Make a smooth layer of beans in the bottom of a clear container with a tight-fitting lid. (Save the rest of the beans to make a burrito, pages 34–35.) Cover with a layer of guacamole and then a layer of sour cream. Continue layering with the tomato, lettuce, and cheese. Cover tightly and refrigerate until ready to go. Pack tortilla chips in a bag for scooping.

**FOR THE GUACAMOLE**

**ripe avocado** ½, diced

**fresh lime juice** 1 teaspoon

**ground cumin** ¼ teaspoon

**salt and ground pepper**

**refried beans** ¼ cup (2 oz/60 g)

**sour cream or plain yogurt** ¼ cup (2 oz/60 g)

**plum tomato** 1, diced

**lettuce** ¼ cup (⅓ oz/10 g) shredded

**Cheddar cheese** ¼ cup (1 oz/30 g) shredded

**tortilla chips, homemade (page 81) or purchased**

**MAKES 1 SERVING**

### substitution, please!

**If creamy stuff isn't their scene:** omit the sour cream.
**If green stuff doesn't fly:** omit the guacamole and substitute sliced black olives for the lettuce.
**If tomatoes make them gag:** substitute chopped red bell pepper.

# go-to bean dips

## lemony hummus

Pour 1 can (15 oz/470 g) chickpeas into a sieve set over a small bowl. Measure out ¼ cup (2 fl oz/60 ml) of the bean liquid and reserve; discard the remaining liquid. Place the chickpeas in a blender or food processor. Add 2 tablespoons tahini; 2 tablespoons fresh lemon juice; ½ teaspoon cumin; 1 teaspoon salt; 1 clove garlic, chopped; and the reserved chickpea liquid and blend until smooth. With the machine running, slowly drizzle in ¼ cup (2 fl oz/60 ml) olive oil and continue to blend until very smooth. Pack each serving in a small airtight container and close tightly. Refrigerate until ready to go. Makes about 2 cups (16 oz/500 g).

## herbed white bean dip

Place 1 can (15 oz/470 g) cannellini beans, rinsed and drained, in a blender or food processor. Add 1 shallot, chopped; 2 teaspoons minced fresh rosemary (or 1 teaspoon dried); 2 teaspoons fresh lemon juice; ¼ teaspoon salt; and a few grindings of pepper and blend until smooth. With the machine running, slowly drizzle in 2 tablespoons olive oil and continue to blend until the mixture is very smooth. Pack each serving in a small airtight container and close tightly. Refrigerate until ready to go. Makes about 2 cups (16 oz/500 g).

### fresh veggie dippers

Any of the home-baked dippers on the opposite page, as well as the fresh ones listed below, will go great with these bean dips.

- Green, red, yellow, and/or orange bell pepper strips
- Broccoli florets
- Carrot or celery sticks
- Cherry tomatoes
- Cucumber spears
- Sugar snap peas
- Zucchini sticks

# home-baked dippers

## tortilla chips

Preheat the broiler. Brush both sides of 4 corn tortillas with olive oil. Cut each tortilla into 8 triangles, or cut out shapes using a cookie cutter. Spread the triangles in a single layer on a baking sheet and sprinkle with salt. Toast, turning once, until golden and crisp, 3–5 minutes. Let cool.

## pita chips

Preheat the broiler. Split two 6-inch (15-cm) pita breads in half to create 4 thin rounds. Brush both sides of the rounds with olive oil. Cut each round into 8 triangles. Spread the triangles in a single layer on a baking sheet and sprinkle with salt. Toast, turning once, until golden and crisp, about 3 minutes. Let cool.

## root veggie chips

Preheat the oven to 500°F (260°C). Lightly grease a baking sheet with olive oil. Peel and thinly slice 2 or 3 beets or carrots (or 1 of each). Arrange the slices in a single layer on the prepared sheet. Drizzle with olive oil and sprinkle with salt. Bake, turning once, until crisp, about 20 minutes. Transfer to paper towels to drain.

## sweet potato chips

Preheat the oven to 500°F (260°C). Lightly grease a baking sheet with olive oil. Peel 2 sweet potatoes. Halve each lengthwise, then thinly slice crosswise. Arrange the slices in a single layer on the sheet. Drizzle with olive oil and sprinkle with salt. Bake, turning once, until crisp, about 20 minutes. Transfer to paper towels to drain.

# on the sweet side

----------------------------------------

### vanilla-raspberry dip

Fill a small airtight container about halfway with vanilla yogurt. Top with a thin, smooth layer of raspberry jam. Add another layer of yogurt. Top the yogurt with a spiral or smiley face of jam, if you like. Close tightly and refrigerate until ready to go. Pack sliced or skewered fruit dippers (see below) along with the dip. Makes 1 serving.

### honey-granola dip

Fill a small airtight container about halfway with plain or vanilla yogurt. Add a layer of granola, and then another layer of yogurt. Top with a generous drizzle of honey and a sprinkling of granola. Close tightly and refrigerate until ready to go. Pack sliced or skewered fruit dippers (see below) along with the dip. Makes 1 serving.

## fruity dippers

- Fresh apple slices or dried apple chips
- Dried apricots
- Dried banana chips
- Fresh berries or grapes skewered onto toothpicks
- Dried mango strips
- Cantaloupe or honeydew melon slices
- Fresh peach or nectarine slices
- Fresh pineapple wedges
- Halved strawberries

# snackarama

Grab-and-go snacks are a great way to fill out a lunch box. They also double as yummy after-school bites and playdate offerings. Plus, preparing any of the recipes in this chapter can be a fun mom-and-me activity.

celery with nut butter or cream cheese and raisins

mini pretzels or pretzel sticks

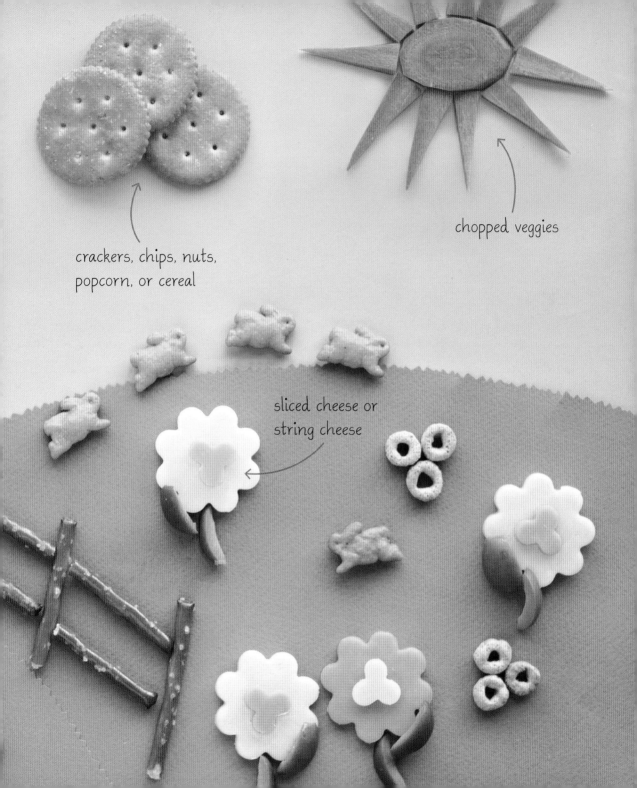

crackers, chips, nuts,
popcorn, or cereal

chopped veggies

sliced cheese or
string cheese

# deviled eggs

Place the eggs on a cutting board. Cut each egg in half lengthwise. Using a spoon, scoop out the yolks and transfer to a bowl.

Add the mayonnaise and mustard to the bowl with the yolks. Use the spoon to mash them all together into a smooth paste. Season to taste with salt and pepper.

Carefully scoop a small mound of the yolk mixture back into each egg white half. Sprinkle each deviled egg with a pinch of paprika. Pack into airtight containers. Cover tightly and refrigerate until ready to go.

**hard-boiled eggs (page 105)** 2, peeled

**mayonnaise** 1 tablespoon

**Dijon mustard** ¼ teaspoon

**salt and ground pepper**

**paprika** 4 small pinches

**MAKES 4 DEVILED EGG HALVES**

## mix it up

- Stir in chopped green onion, minced fresh herbs, grated lemon zest, chopped dill pickles, or chopped capers.
- Omit the mustard and substitute ¼ teaspoon curry powder or ground cumin.
- For crunch, sprinkle cracker crumbs or cooked, crumbled bacon over the finished eggs.

Pack the eggs with a simple
salad to round out the meal.

# skewer mania

Boost the fun factor of
any food exponentially
by threading it on a stic

## mozzarella, cantaloupe & prosciutto

Have ready short wooden skewers or
toothpicks. Working with 1 skewer at
a time, alternately thread small cubes
of cantaloupe, fresh mozzarella balls
(called *bocconcini*), and rolled-up
pieces of prosciutto onto each skewer.
Substitute grapes or cherry tomatoes for
the cantaloupe, if you like.

## ham & pineapple

Have ready short wooden skewers
or toothpicks. Working with 1 skewer
at a time, alternately thread pineapple
chunks and ham pieces onto each
skewer. Substitute cooked sausage
slices for the ham, if you like.

## salami, olive & string cheese

Have ready short wooden skewers or toothpicks. Cut a string cheese stick crosswise into small pieces. Working with 1 skewer at a time, alternately thread rolled-up slices of salami, cubes of cheese, and pitted black or green olives onto each skewer. Substitute any cubed cheese for the string cheese.

## chicken & bell pepper with bbq sauce

Have ready short wooden skewers or toothpicks. Working with 1 skewer at a time, alternately thread grilled chicken cubes and chunks of bell pepper onto each skewer. Include a small container of BBQ sauce for dipping.

# pop-your-own popcorn

In a large, heavy saucepan, heat the oil over medium-high heat. Add the popcorn kernels, cover, and cook, shaking the pan often, until you start to hear popping. Continue to cook, shaking the pan constantly, until the popping slows to 3–5 seconds between pops. Remove from the heat and pour the popped popcorn into a bowl.

Drizzle the melted butter, if using, over the popcorn, and sprinkle with ½–1 teaspoon salt. Choose a seasoning from the ideas below, or make up your own flavor combination. Using your hands or a large spoon, toss the popcorn to mix the ingredients evenly. Let popcorn cool completely before packing into snack bags or the steam will cause it to get soggy.

**canola or peanut oil**  2 tablespoons

**popcorn kernels**  ¼ cup
(1½ oz/45 g)

**butter**  2 tablespoons, melted
(optional)

**salt**

**favorite seasonings (see note)**

**MAKES 2-4 SERVINGS**

## seasonings to try

- **garlic butter**  Add 1–2 cloves garlic, minced, to the butter when you melt it.

- **Parmesan**  Sprinkle ½ cup (2 oz/60 g) grated Parmesan cheese over the popcorn after you add the butter and salt.

- **nutritional yeast**  Omit the salt and butter. Sprinkle a little bit of soy sauce and a generous amount of nutritional yeast over the popcorn.

- **cinnamon sugar**  In a small bowl, combine 1 teaspoon sugar and ½ teaspoon cinnamon. Sprinkle the cinnamon sugar over the popcorn after you add the butter and salt.

# sweet-n-salty kettle corn

In a large, heavy saucepan, heat the oil over medium heat. Add the sugar and stir with a wooden spoon just until it begins to bubble, 1–2 minutes. Add the popcorn kernels and stir until well coated with the sugar. Cover tightly and cook, shaking the pan often, until you start to hear popping. Continue to cook, shaking the pan constantly, until the popping slows to 3–5 seconds between pops. If the mixture smells like it's burning, remove the pan from the heat and shake constantly until the kernels stop popping.

Remove the pan from the heat and wait until all popping has stopped. Uncover the pan and, using the wooden spoon, stir the popcorn to coat it evenly with any sugar remaining on the bottom of the pan. Pour the popcorn into a bowl, sprinkle with ½ teaspoon salt, and stir once more to mix. Let popcorn cool completely before packing into snack bags or the steam will cause it to get soggy.

**canola or peanut oil**  2 tablespoons

**sugar**  2 tablespoons

**popcorn kernels**  ¼ cup (1½ oz/45 g)

**salt**

**MAKES 2-4 SERVINGS**

## party time

Consider bringing homemade kettle corn to your child's next class party. It's a festive, low-sugar, and inexpensive way to feed an entire classroom for a special event. Find some decorative bags or cups for serving, or make your own bags with parchment paper and fun stickers.

# homemade granola bars

Preheat the oven to 350°F (180°C). Line a 9-inch (23-cm) square pan with a large sheet of waxed paper that's been greased on both sides, making sure to leave a generous border of paper above the pan rim.

In a large bowl, combine the coconut and cranberries; set aside. On a rimmed baking sheet, combine the oats, wheat germ, almonds, and sunflower seeds. Bake the oat mixture until toasted and fragrant, 5–10 minutes. Remove from the oven. Add the hot oat mixture to the fruit-coconut mixture and stir until combined.

In a saucepan, melt the 2 tablespoons butter over medium heat. Add the brown sugar, honey, vanilla, cinnamon, and salt and stir until the sugar dissolves, about 5 minutes. Bring to a boil, then remove from the heat and pour over the fruit-oat mixture.

Using a large spoon, gently stir together all the ingredients until well combined. Scoop the mixture into the prepared pan. Place a sheet of waxed paper on top and, using your hands, firmly press the mixture into the pan, making a compact, even layer. Let the mixture set in the pan until completely cool, about 10 minutes.

Remove the top sheet of waxed paper. Grab the sides of the bottom sheet of waxed paper and lift the firmed oat mixture from the pan. Cut into squares or triangles. Pack 1 or 2 into small snack bags. (The remaining bars can be stored in an airtight container for up to 5 days, or frozen for up to 1 month.)

**butter** 2 tablespoons, plus softened butter for greasing

**shredded coconut** 1 cup (4 oz/125 g)

**dried cranberries, dried cherries, or chopped dried apricots** 1 cup (4 oz/125 g)

**old-fashioned rolled oats** 2 cups (6 oz/185 g)

**wheat germ** 1 cup (3 oz/90 g)

**whole almonds, cashews, or peanuts** 1 cup (5½ oz/170 g)

**shelled sunflower seeds or mini chocolate chips** 1 cup (4 oz/125 g)

**brown sugar** 1 cup (7 oz/220 g) firmly packed

**honey** ½ cup (6 oz/185 g)

**vanilla extract** 1 teaspoon

**ground cinnamon** 1 teaspoon

**salt** ¼ teaspoon

**MAKES ABOUT 16 PIECES**

sunflower seeds

coconut flakes

almonds

mini chocolate chips

banana chips

# trail mix
## Make your own blend of nuts, seeds, dried fruit, and other wholesome bite-sized ingredients

popcorn

dried mango

cashews

sesame sticks

dried cranberries

dried apricots

pecans

dried cherries

yogurt-covered raisins

raisins

peanuts

wasabi peas

**groovy combos**

almonds
dried cherries
yogurt-covered raisins
sunflower seeds
mini chocolate chips

popcorn
peanuts
fish-shaped crackers
mini pretzels
dried edamame

dried mango
banana chips
cashews
coconut flakes
mini chocolate chips

wasabi peas
peanuts
sesame sticks
sunflower seeds
dried pineapple

# ultimate munchie mix

Preheat the oven to 250°F (120°C). Put the butter in a shallow baking dish and set in the oven just until melted. Stir in the Worcestershire sauce, sugar, salt, onion powder, and garlic powder until well blended. Add the cereal, pretzels, and nuts and toss gently but thoroughly to coat with the seasoned butter.

Spread the mixture evenly in the dish. Bake, stirring every 10 minutes, until crisp, about 45 minutes. Let cool completely. Pack handfuls of the mix into airtight containers or snack bags. (Store the remaining mix in an airtight container at room temperature for up to 1 week.)

**unsalted butter**  1 tablespoon

**Worcestershire sauce**  1 teaspoon

**sugar**  ½ teaspoon

**salt**  ¼ teaspoon

**onion powder**  ⅛ teaspoon

**garlic powder**  ⅛ teaspoon

**Chex cereal**  1 cup (3 oz/90 g)

**mini pretzels or bite-sized crackers**
½ cup (1½ oz/45 g)

**mixed nuts**  ¼ cup (1 oz/30 g)

**MAKES 3 OR 4 SERVINGS**

## sell it!

Use goldfish-shaped crackers to make this crunchy mixture well-nigh irresistible to the under-ten set. For a nut-free, sweet-and-salty version, replace the nuts with raisins, dried cranberries, or dried cherries.

# nutty cereal balls

In a small saucepan, combine the honey and brown sugar and heat over medium heat, stirring, until the mixture begins to boil and the brown sugar dissolves, 2–3 minutes. Remove from the heat. Add the peanut butter and stir until blended and smooth. Add the cereal and stir gently until evenly coated.

Lightly grease a rimmed baking sheet with butter. Using a spoon, scoop up a tablespoon or so of the cereal mixture and use your hands to press it into a 1½-inch (4-cm) ball. Place the ball on the baking sheet. Continue to scoop and mold the remaining cereal mixture into balls, placing them evenly apart on the baking sheet. Place the baking sheet in the refrigerator and chill the balls until set, 5–10 minutes. Pack 1 or 2 into snack bags. (Store the remaining balls in an airtight container at room temperature for up to 3 days.)

**honey** 2 tablespoons

**brown sugar** 1 tablespoon

**creamy peanut butter or almond butter** 2 tablespoons

**puffed rice cereal** 1 cup (3 oz/90 g)

**butter** for greasing

**MAKES ABOUT 10 BALLS**

### cereal ball savvy

If the mixture is too sticky to easily shape into balls, pop it in the fridge for 10 minutes to chill it. If you want a smoother texture, put the rice cereal in a plastic bag and crush it a bit before adding it to the peanut butter mixture.

Cutting the corn bread into sticks makes it ideal for dipping

# cheesy corn bread sticks

Preheat the oven to 425°F (220°C). Lightly grease a 9-by-13-inch (23-by-33-cm) baking pan with butter.

In a large bowl, stir together the cornmeal, flour, sugar, baking powder, baking soda, and salt. In another bowl, whisk together the sour cream, eggs, milk, and melted butter until blended. Add the wet ingredients to the dry ingredients and stir until smooth. Stir in the corn kernels. Spread the batter evenly in the prepared pan. Sprinkle with the cheese.

Bake until the corn bread is golden brown and a toothpick inserted into the center comes out clean, about 20 minutes. Let cool slightly in the pan on a wire rack. Cut the corn bread into finger-sized sticks and pack into snack bags. (Wrap the remaining corn bread sticks in foil, then place in a zippered plastic bag and refrigerate for up to 5 days or freeze for up to 2 months.)

**unsalted butter** 4 tablespoons (2 oz/60 g), melted, plus softened butter for greasing

**yellow cornmeal** 1 cup (5 oz/155 g)

**flour** 1 cup (5 oz/155 g)

**light brown sugar** 3 tablespoons firmly packed

**baking powder** 1 teaspoon

**baking soda** 1 teaspoon

**salt** ½ teaspoon

**sour cream** 1 cup (8 oz/250 g)

**large eggs** 2

**milk** ¼ cup (2 fl oz/60 ml)

**corn kernels** 1½ cups (9 oz/280 g), thawed if frozen

**Cheddar cheese** ¾ cup (3 oz/90 g) shredded

**MAKES 4-6 SERVINGS**

# banana bread

Preheat the oven to 350°F (180°C). Butter and flour two 3-by-5½-inch (7.5-by-14-cm) mini loaf pans or one 5-by-9-inch (13-by-23-cm) standard loaf pan. In a medium bowl, mix together the flour, sugar, baking soda, and salt. In a large bowl, mash the bananas well with a fork. Add the ½ cup melted butter, the eggs, yogurt, and vanilla. Stir until blended. Gradually add the flour mixture, stirring gently, just until mixed. Scrape the batter into the prepared loaf pans, dividing evenly.

Bake until a toothpick inserted into the center comes out clean, about 40 minutes for the mini loaves or about 1 hour for the larger loaf. If the top begins to brown too much during baking, cover loosely with aluminum foil. Let the pan cool on a wire rack for 10 minutes, then turn the bread out onto the rack, turn right side up, and let cool completely. Cut the bread into slices and pack into snack bags. (Wrap the remaining bread in foil, then place in a zippered plastic bag and refrigerate for up to 5 days or freeze for up to 2 months.)

**butter** ½ cup (4 oz/125 g), melted, plus softened butter for greasing

**all-purpose flour** 2¼ cups (11½ oz/360 g), plus more for dusting the pan

**sugar** 1 cup (8 oz/250 g)

**baking soda** 1 teaspoon

**salt** ½ teaspoon

**very ripe bananas** 3

**large eggs** 2, lightly beaten

**plain yogurt** ⅓ cup (3 oz/90 g)

**vanilla extract** 1 teaspoon

**MAKES 2 MINI LOAVES OR 1 LARGE LOAF**

## easy to freeze

If you have a lot of ripe bananas lying around, make 2 loaves of this bread and freeze one for later. Cool the loaf completely, wrap in plastic wrap or foil, and place in a large zippered plastic bag. Freeze for up to 2 months. Let thaw at room temperature overnight before packing.

Make a tempting banana-bread sandwich with whipped cream cheese (or nut butter) and honey.

# smoothies
### Thick, colorful fruit drinks to brighten up the morning rush

### green machine

In a blender, combine 1 cup (2 oz/60 g) chopped spinach or kale; ¾ cup (6 fl oz/180 ml) apple or orange juice; ½ banana, peeled and sliced; ½ apple, peeled and diced; and 3 ice cubes. Cover and blend on high speed until smooth.

### strawberry-banana

In a blender, combine 4–6 fresh or frozen strawberries; ½ cup (4 fl oz/125 ml) orange juice; ½ banana, peeled and sliced; ¼ cup (2 oz/60 g) plain or vanilla yogurt; and 3 ice cubes (if using fresh fruit). Cover and blend on high speed until smooth.

Pack in a pre-chilled insulated container and include a straw for easy drinking.

### berrylicious

In a blender, combine 1 cup (4 oz/125 g) fresh or frozen blueberries, raspberries, and/or strawberries; ½ cup (4 fl oz/125 ml) cran-raspberry juice; ¼ cup (2 oz/60 g) plain or vanilla yogurt; and 3 ice cubes (if using fresh fruit). Cover and blend on high speed until smooth.

### peachy keen

In a blender, combine ½ cup (3 oz/90 g) fresh or frozen peach chunks; ½ cup (4 fl oz/125 ml) apple juice; ½ banana, peeled and sliced; ¼ cup (2 oz/60 g) vanilla yogurt; and 3 ice cubes (if using fresh fruit). Cover and blend on high speed until smooth.

# cooking basics

Everyone agrees that packing a lunch should take as little time—and dirty as few dishes—as possible. But there are a few key lunch-box staples that are worth the time it takes to cook them, whether you do them in advance or make time in the morning.

## blanching fresh or frozen vegetables

Bring a saucepan of water to a boil over high heat, and prepare a bowl of ice water. When the water comes to a boil, add fresh or frozen vegetables and cook just until tender-crisp (if fresh) or just until warmed through (if frozen), 3–5 minutes. Drain the vegetables and immediately transfer them to the ice water to stop the cooking. Drain again.

## cooking chicken breasts

You can cook up a few skinless, boneless chicken breast halves in just 10 minutes or less. Cook the meat using one of the methods below, let the meat cool, and then shred or chop as needed.

**poaching** Bring a large saucepan of water to a boil over high heat. Add ½ teaspoon salt and the chicken, reduce the heat until the water is barely simmering, and cook until the chicken is opaque throughout, 8–10 minutes.

**sautéing** Season both sides of each chicken breast half with salt and pepper. In a frying pan, heat a thin film of canola or olive oil over medium heat. Add the chicken and cook, turning once, until golden brown on the outside and opaque in the center, 4–5 minutes per side.

## cooking pasta

Because the cooking time for pasta varies with the shape and type of noodle, it's best to follow the cooking instructions on the package. Remember to stir the pasta occasionally as it cooks, and test it often to make sure you don't overcook it. To prevent the noodles from sticking together as they cool, coat them with pasta sauce or a little olive oil immediately after cooking.

## cooking rice

**white rice** The exact ratio of water to rice varies with different types of rice, but here are general directions for cooking rice on the stove top: For 3 cups (15 oz/470 g) cooked rice, place 1 cup (7 oz/220 g) uncooked rice in a fine-mesh sieve and rinse until the water runs clear. Transfer the rice to a heavy saucepan and add 1½ cups (12 fl oz/375 ml) water. Bring to a boil, give the rice a quick stir, reduce the heat to low, cover, and cook, undisturbed, until all the water has been absorbed, about 20 minutes.

**brown rice** Follow the instructions for white rice, but increase the cooking time to 40 minutes.

**sushi rice** Follow the cooking instructions for white rice, being sure to use short-grain (sushi) rice. While the rice cooks, combine ¼ cup (2 fl oz/60 ml) rice vinegar, 3 tablespoons sugar, and 1 tablespoon salt in a small saucepan over low heat and cook, stirring, until the sugar and

salt dissolve, about 2 minutes.
Let cool. Transfer the cooked rice
to a wide, shallow dish and use a
spatula to spread it out evenly.
Slowly pour in the vinegar
mixture while slicing the spatula
through the rice; do not stir.
Cover with a damp kitchen towel
until ready to roll out your sushi.

## frying bacon

In a frying pan, cook strips
of bacon over medium heat,
turning once, until crisp and
browned, about 6 minutes.
Transfer to a paper towel–lined
plate to drain.

## hard-boiling eggs

Put the eggs in a small saucepan
and add cold water to cover.
Place over high heat and bring
the water to a boil. Reduce the
heat to medium-low and simmer
the eggs for 12 minutes. Place
the saucepan in the sink and run
cold water over the eggs to cool
them. Roll each egg on a work
surface to crack the eggshell.
Carefully peel off the shell.

### get a jump on the week

A little bit of time—even 10 minutes—spent during the weekend
to prepare for the week's lunches will pay off big during the week.
Making time for prep work also means spending less money on
presliced, prewashed, or premade foods.

- Wash and chop veggies
  and store them in small bags
  or containers to use as
  dippers or to incorporate into
  sandwiches and wraps.

- Cut fresh fruit like pineapple,
  melon, or mango into cubes
  or spears for grab-and-go
  lunch packing.

- Wash and spin-dry lettuce.

- Make a simple dip (see pages
  76 and 80) to pack with
  veggies, chips, or crackers.
  You can also bake your own
  healthy chips (page 81).

- Whip up a homemade snack,
  like trail mix (page 94),
  popcorn (page 90), or granola
  bars (page 93).

- Prepare a batch of pesto
  (page 67) to mix with
  precooked pasta.

- Make a vinaigrette or other
  salad dressing.

- Make a batch of oatmeal
  (page 59) big enough for a few
  breakfasts and/or lunches.

- Roast or grill vegetables like
  corn on the cob, bell pepper,
  tomato, and zucchini to use in
  pasta (page 51) or a frittata.

- Cook a chicken breast or a
  few strips of bacon for use in
  salads, wraps, or sandwiches
  during the week.

- Hard-boil eggs to have on
  hand to make quick work of
  deviled eggs or egg salad; to
  slice for salads; or to eat as is.

- Precook rice or pasta to use
  as a base for a hearty lunch.

- Make a soup (page 60) or
  batch of chili (page 63).

# use it or lose it

Maybe you hard-boiled a few eggs over the weekend; or you have leftover cooked chicken and rice from last night's dinner; or perhaps you spy some bananas languishing on the counter. Here's a list of recipes that will help you use up ingredients that won't last forever.

**cooked vegetables**
- super veggie burrito (page 35)
- orzo & grilled veggie salad (page 51)
- stealth side salads (page 52)
- mac & cheese, all dressed up (page 64)
- wagon wheels with pesto & broccoli (page 67)
- teriyaki rice bowl (page 68)

**cooked chicken**
- zesty chicken salad pita pockets (page 25)
- chicken & rice burrito (page 35)
- chicken & rice wrap with peanut dip (page 37)
- chopped caesar salad (page 44)
- asian chicken salad (page 45)
- chicken florentine mac & cheese (page 65)

- teriyaki rice bowl (page 68)
- chicken & bell pepper skewers with bbq sauce (page 89)

**roast turkey breast**
- classic turkey club (page 16)
- thanksgiving special (page 19)

**cooked steak or pork**
- philly cheesesteak roll (page 20)
- steak & salsa verde burrito (page 35)
- pork & chile burrito (page 35)
- teriyaki rice bowl (page 68)

**cooked tofu**
- five-spice tofu roll (page 20)
- teriyaki rice bowl (page 68)

**cooked bacon**
- classic turkey club (page 16)
- blt wrap (page 32)
- mac & cheese with bacon & green onion (page 65)

**cooked rice**
- burrito in a bowl (page 35)
- chicken & rice wrap with peanut dip (page 37)
- veggie sushi rolls (page 40)
- teriyaki rice bowl (page 68)
- oh-so-simple fried rice (page 70)

**cooked pasta**
- orzo & grilled veggie salad (page 51)
- peanut butter noodles with snow peas (page 54)
- wagon wheels with pesto & broccoli (page 67)

**hard-boiled eggs**
- egg salad on mini bagels (page 22)
- deviled eggs (page 86)

**overripe bananas**
- banana bread (page 100)
- smoothies (page 102)

# index

# weldon**owen**

415 Jackson Street, Suite 200, San Francisco, CA 94111
Telephone: 415 291 0100  Fax: 415 291 8841
www.wopublishing.com

**THE LUNCH BOX**
Conceived and produced by Weldon Owen, Inc.
Copyright © 2011 Weldon Owen, Inc.

Color separations by Embassy Graphics
Printed and bound in China by 1010 Printing

First printed in 2011
10 9 8 7 6 5 4 3 2

Library of Congress Control Number: 2011924279

ISBN-13: 978-1-61628-122-9
ISBN-10: 1-61628-122-7

Weldon Owen is a division of

# BONNIER

**WELDON OWEN, INC.**
**CEO and President** Terry Newell
**VP, Sales and Marketing** Amy Kaneko
**Director of Finance** Mark Perrigo

**VP and Publisher** Hannah Rahill
**Associate Editor** Julia Nelson

**Creative Director** Emma Boys
**Senior Designer** Ashley Lima

**Production Director** Chris Hemesath
**Production Manager** Michelle Duggan
**Color Manager** Teri Bell

**Photographer** Emma Boys
**Food Stylist** Kim Laidlaw
**Prop Stylist** Leigh Noe
**Illustrations** Diana Heom

**ACKNOWLEDGMENTS**
Weldon Owen would like to thank the following people for their generous support in making this book:
Leslie Evans, Carrie Neves, Jennifer Newens, Elizabeth Parson, and Tracy White Taylor.

## about the authors

**Kate McMillan** is a chef, cooking instructor, and owner of an eponymous catering company. She lives in Northern California with her husband and three young daughters, who were tireless taste-testers for this book.

**Sarah Putman Clegg** is a freelance editor, writer, and author of *Love in Spoonfuls*. She lives in the San Francisco Bay Area with her husband and young son, who eats things from his lunch box that he would never consume in her presence.